How To Create A Successful Product That Customers Will Want

Techniques For Product Managers To Boost Product Sales And Increase Customer Satisfaction

"Practical, proven techniques that will help you to make your product management job a success"

Dr. Jim Anderson

Published by:
Blue Elephant Consulting
Tampa, Florida

Copyright © 2016 by Dr. Jim Anderson

All rights reserved. No part of this book may be reproduced of transmitted in any form or by any means, electronic or mechanical, including photocopying, recording or by any information storage and retrieval system without written permission of the publisher, except for inclusion of brief quotations in a review.

Printed in the United States of America

Library of Congress Control Number: 2016954858

ISBN-13: 978-1539020240
ISBN-10: 153902024X

Warning – Disclaimer

The purpose of this book is to educate and entertain. This book does not promise or guarantee that anyone following the ideas, tips, suggestions, techniques or strategies will be successful. The author, publisher and distributor(s) shall have neither liability nor responsibility to anyone with respect to any loss or damage caused, or alleged to be caused, directly or indirectly by the information contained in this book.

Recent Books By The Author

Product Management

- What Product Managers Need To Know About World-Class Product Development: How Product Managers Can Create Successful Products

- How Product Managers Can Learn To Understand Their Customers: Techniques For Product Managers To Better Understand What Their Customers Really Want

Public Speaking

- Tools Speakers Need In Order To Give The Perfect Speech: What tools to use to create your next speech so that your message will be remembered forever!

- How To Create A Speech That Will Be Remembered

CIO Skills

- **Becoming A Powerful And Effective Leader: Tips And Techniques That IT Managers Can Use In Order To Develop Leadership Skills**

- CIO Secrets For Growing Innovation: Tips And Techniques For CIOs To Use In Order To Make Innovation Happen In Their IT Department

IT Manager Skills

- Save Yourself, Save Your Job – How To Manage Your IT Career: Secrets That IT Managers Can Use In Order To Have A Successful Career

- Growing Your CIO Career: How CIOs Can Work With The Entire Company In Order To Be Successful

Negotiating

- Take No Prisoners In Your Next Negotiation: How To Start A Negotiation In Order To Get The Best Possible Outcome

- Learn How To Signal In Your Next Negotiation: How To Develop The Skill Of Effective Signaling In A Negotiation In Order To Get The Best Possible Outcome

Note: See a complete list of books by Dr. Jim Anderson at the back of this book.

Acknowledgements

Any book like this one is the result of years of real-world work experience. In my over 25 years of working for 7 different firms, I have met countless fantastic people and I've been mentored by some truly exceptional ones. Although I've probably forgotten some of the people who made me the person that I am today, here is my attempt to finally give them the recognition that they so truly deserve:

- Thomas P. Anderson
- Art Puett
- Bobbi Marshall
- Bob Boggs

Dr. Jim Anderson

This book is dedicated to my wife Lori. None of this would have been possible without her love and support.

Thanks for the best 21 years of my life (so far)...!

Table Of Contents

WHAT MAKES A PRODUCT SUCCESSFUL? 8

ABOUT THE AUTHOR 10

CHAPTER 1: SUCCESSFUL PRODUCT MANGERS ARE GOOD LOOKERS 15

CHAPTER 2: WHO'S EVER SEEN A GREEN PRODUCT MANAGER? 18

CHAPTER 3: PRODUCT MANGERS KNOW THAT GREEN PRODUCTS COST MORE – FOR AWHILE 21

CHAPTER 4: GREEN PRODUCT MANGERS HAVE GREEN BOSSES 24

CHAPTER 5: PRODUCT MANAGERS KNOW THAT EVERYBODY MUST BE GREEN 27

CHAPTER 6: WHAT A PASTRY STORE CAN TEACH PRODUCT MANAGERS 30

CHAPTER 7: PRODUCT MANAGER LESSONS FROM AN ONLINE COMPANY IN CHINA 34

CHAPTER 8: PERFORMANCE BASED PRICING – IS IT RIGHT FOR PRODUCT MANAGERS IN TOUGH TIMES? 37

CHAPTER 9: GOING CHEAP IS OK FOR SOME PRODUCT MANAGERS 42

CHAPTER 10: NEW COKE: A PRODUCT MANAGER CAMPFIRE STORY 45

CHAPTER 11: COST OF MATERIALS IS A PRODUCT MANAGER'S NEW FRIEND 49

CHAPTER 12: SLIMMED DOWN PRODUCTS MAKE PRODUCT MANAGERS LOOK GOOD 53

What Makes A Product Successful?

The success of a product manager is judged by the success of their product. This of course leads to the question, what does it take to have a successful product? One of the most important things is how a product manager chooses to look at their market: do they take the short term view or the long term view?

One of the biggest decisions that modern product managers have to make these days is if they want their product to "go green". Becoming environmentally aware and perhaps modifying how your product is made or sold can be an expensive undertaking. However, if your customers are the type that are looking for products that won't harm the environment, then perhaps this is a step that you are going to have to investigate taking.

No product manager has all of the answers. What this means for us is that we need to keep our eyes open and go looking for success stories that we can find. These successful products have a lesson to teach us if only we'd be willing to listen to them. No matter if we're looking at successful pastry shop or an online company in China, there are lessons for all of us here.

One of the most difficult tasks associated with being a product manager is coming up with the right price for your product. There are a number of different ways to go about doing this and performance-based pricing is one of them. However, you're going to have to ask yourself if this is the right thing to do in tough times.

Another approach to solving the pricing puzzle that some product managers take is to go cheap. This can have an impact on your product and how your customers view both your product and your company. If you choose to take this route, you'll need to move carefully.

In the world of product mangers there are many stories that we tell amongst ourselves whenever product managers get together. One of the most famous of these stories is the tale of "New Coke". What should have been a big success turned into a massive failure and why this happened is important to all of us.

For more information on what it takes to be a great product manager, check out my blog, The Accidental Product Manager, at:

www.TheAccidentalPM.com

Good luck!

- Dr. Jim Anderson

About The Author

I must confess that I never set out to be a product manager. When I went to school, I studied Computer Science and thought that I'd get a nice job programming and that would be that. Well, at least part of that plan worked out!

My first job was working for Boeing on their F/A-18 fighter jet program. I spent my days programming fighter jet software in assembly language and I loved it. The U.S. government decided to save some money and went looking for other countries to sell this plane to. This put me into an unfamiliar role: I started to meet with foreign military officials in order to explain what my product did.

Time moved on and so did I. I found myself working for Siemens, the big German telecommunications company. They were making phone switches and selling them to the seven U.S. phone companies. The problem was that the switches were too complicated. Customers couldn't tell the difference between one complicated phone switch from another complicated phone switch.

The Siemens sales folks were in a bind. They didn't know enough about how the switches worked to tell their customers why they should buy them. Siemens reached out into their engineering unit looking for anyone who could help the sales teams out. I put my hand up and overnight I became a product manager.

Since then I've spent over 20 years working as a product manager for both big companies and startups. This has given me an opportunity to do everything that a product manager does many, many times. I know what works as well as what doesn't work.

I now live in Tampa Florida where I spend my time managing my consulting business, Blue Elephant Consulting, teaching college courses at the University of South Florida, and traveling to work with companies like yours to share the knowledge that I have about how product managers can make their product be a success.

I'm always available to answer questions and I can be reached at:

Dr. Jim Anderson
Blue Elephant Consulting
Email: jim@BlueElephantConsulting.com
Facebook: http://goo.gl/1TVoK
Web: **www.BlueElephantConsulting.com**

"Unforgettable communication skills that will set your ideas free..."

Create Products Your Customers Want At A Price That They Are Willing To Pay!

Dr. Jim Anderson is available to provide training and coaching on the two topics that are the most important to product managers everywhere: how do I create the products that my customers want and what should I price them at?

Dr. Anderson believes that in order to both learn and remember what he says, product managers need to laugh. Each one of his speeches is full of fun and humor so that what he says "sticks" with everyone.

Dr. Anderson's Product Management Training Includes:

1. How can you segment your market?
2. What problems are your customers having right now?
3. Which of your customer's problems does your product solve?
4. How much of this problem does your product solve?
5. How much will it cost your customer if they don't fix this problem?

Dr. Jim Anderson presents over 100 speeches per year. To invite Dr. Anderson to speak at your event, contact him at:

Phone: 813-418-6970 or
Email: jim@BlueElephantConsulting.com

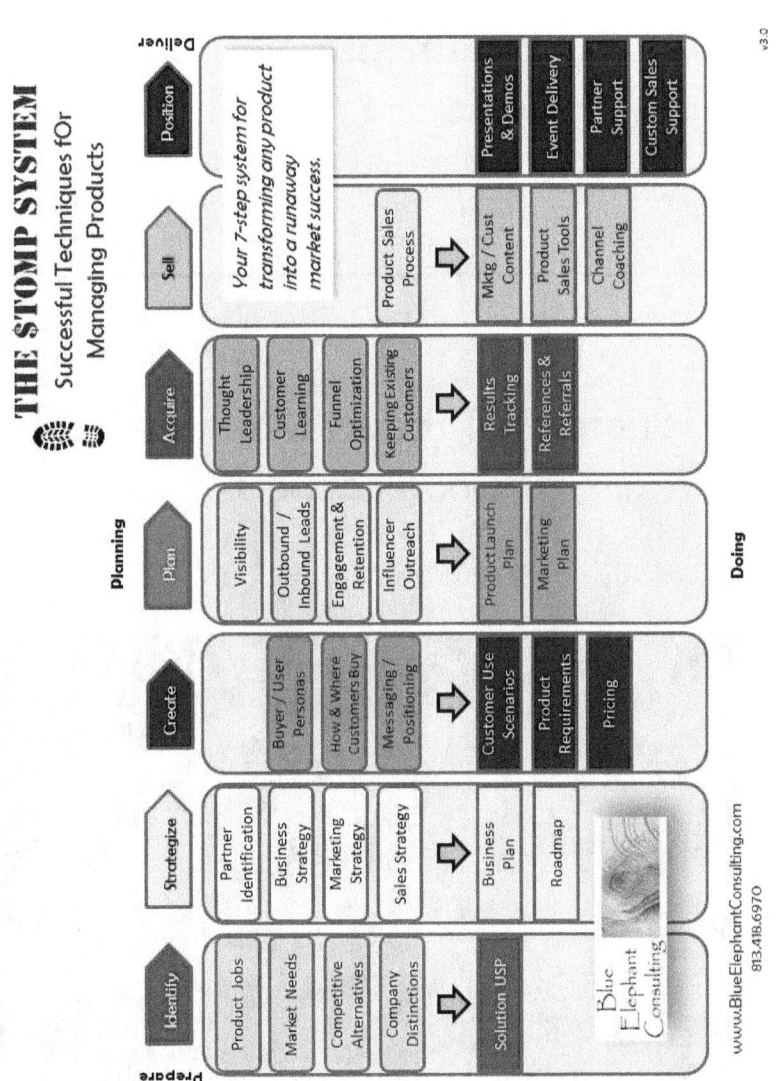

The **$TOMP™** product management system has been created by **Blue Elephant Consulting** to help product managers know what to do and when to do it in order for a product to be successful. Contact us for more information on how you can learn more.

Chapter 1

Successful Product Mangers Are Good Lookers

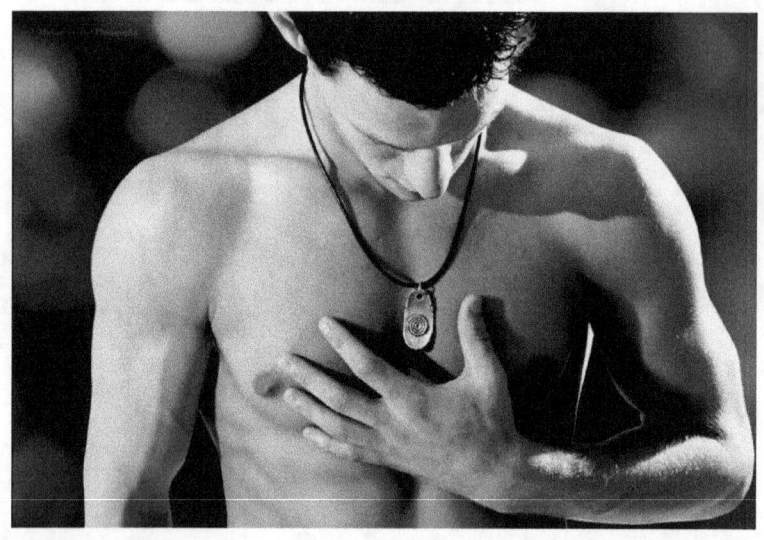

Chapter 1: Successful Product Mangers Are Good Lookers

No, no, we're not talking about being physically attractive here – although... What I'm really getting ready to talk about is the secret to how product managers who work in the rough-and-tumble economies of emerging markets **survive in the long term**. What's their secret and how can we use it to survive the current recession?

Martin Roth and Richard Ettenson over at the Wall Street Journal have been doing some digging in order to find out how product managers can **make the best of tumultuous times**. What they've found is that the ultimate secret to product manager success is to learn to look at the market differently.

Look at the market? Isn't that what you are currently doing each and every day? Probably not. What I'm talking about here is learning to take **a very broad view** of the market that your product(s) are competing in.

I'm sure that you are keeping an eye on the status of your competitors. However, are you monitoring the market's **overall economic data**? The reason that you should be doing this is because it will allow you to figure out where your overall market is headed.

If you can learn to better predict where your market is going, then this will give you an opportunity to decide when it is the best time to **switch from one product strategy to another**. If you can guess this correctly, then you'll be able to use the changes in the market to outflank your competitors.

Roth and Ettenson point out the case of a telephone company in the Dominican Republic that survived economic turmoil back in 2004. They started tracking inflation, unemployment, the exchange rate, etc. in order to better predict **where the local economy was going**. When the prediction was down, they cut product prices and focused on customer retention. When the prediction was up, they raised prices and went after new customers.

Chapter 2

Who's Ever Seen A Green Product Manager?

Chapter 2: Who's Ever Seen A Green Product Manager?

Ok, I'll admit it – sometimes I throw away a plastic bottle that I know could have been recycled. I do it just because it's too much effort to walk the extra distance to hunt down the recycle bin and put it where it's supposed to go. So if I'm willing to sin this much, is there any hope for us product mangers to ever "**go green**"?

It turns out that the world of products and product mangers isn't so much driven by a desire to be a good citizen of this planet (something that apparently I still need to learn), but rather by hard, cold **bottom line results**. That being said, some interesting things are starting to happen out there in the marketplace.

Once upon a time everyone thought that if you boosted the quality of your product, then of course you had to raise your prices also. It turns out that not only was this wrong, but it was dead wrong – a bunch of companies showed everyone that they could not only **boost quality but that they could also cut prices**. Case(s) in point: Dell, Apple, Toyota, etc.

Now it's starting to look like we might have to learn this lesson all over when it comes to **going green with our products**.

Here's the secret: if you've been focusing on the costs of making your product more environmentally friendly, then you've been looking in the wrong direction. The trick is to look for ways **to make less of a mess** when your product is being created. Oh, and you service product managers need to get in on this also.

Just in case you think that this really can't be done, think again. The poster child for going green in a big way is a **Subaru plant** located in Indiana. There 3,000 employees make about 800 cars a day. They've been able to reduce the amount of electricity that they use per car by 14% (that's a LOT of electricity) and (here's the big one) they have not shipped any waste to a landfill since 2004.

If a big old car plant can do that, then just imagine what a high tech product team should be able to do.

Chapter 3

Product Mangers Know That Green Products Cost More – For Awhile

Chapter 3: Product Mangers Know That Green Products Cost More – For Awhile

Pity the poor product manager whose firm has decided to do the trendy thing and "go green". Why you say? Simple – going green can boost profits in the long run, but sadly it can **take some serious time before you see results**.

Alan Robinson and Dean Schroeder over at the Wall Street Journal have taken a look at just what happens when a company goes green and they've got **some interesting things** for product mangers to consider.

The first thing that a product manager needs to realize is that it can be very **easy to implement some early green initiatives** for his / her product. Two quick hits can revolve around the amount of energy that is used to create the product (even software products can benefit by turning lights off when nobody is there) and recycling old materials (copies of last version's user guide anyone?).

It's when you knuckle down and take a look at the whole process that you go through to design the product that a green redesign starts to take on some **serious costs**. If you look farther down your supply chain and start to get your suppliers to go green, this could end up costing you more in the short run.

The goal for all product mangers that are thinking about going green is to make sure that any green changes that they make to their products end up leading to either **cost savings or becoming break even**.

A case in point from a Subaru plant in Indiana that went green is that they discovered that all of those little sparks that fly off during the welding of a car are actually little pieces of metal that end up having to be picked up. When they implemented a new green welding process that caused fewer sparks, they **suddenly had to pick up a lot less metal.**

Chapter 4

Green Product Mangers Have Green Bosses

Chapter 4: Green Product Mangers Have Green Bosses

With "going green" being all the rage right now, product managers should give it some serious consideration for their products. Although we all SHOULD want to make the planet a better place for current and future generations to live, from a practical product management point of view having a green product may reduce costs and increase sales. Not bad, eh?

The first thing to realize is that product mangers can't go green all by themselves. This is one area where you really, truly, do need the buy in of your senior management. This is especially critical in two different areas.

The first area that needs upper management participation is to come up with an agreed on way of measuring how green your product is. You've got to do this both before you start and while you are making improvements – both will show you and your customers how far you've come.

Next you need the support of senior management in order to get the cooperation of other departments. Just because you've been bitten by the green bug, does not mean that the folks over in shipping will share your new found outlook on life. Pressure to conform from above will help you to meet your green product goals.

Finally, it's the worker bees that really need to be engaged in turning your product into a green product. A great example of this is to do some dumpster diving where your product is created. By laying out everything that is in the trash containers where you work, you'll discover what is going into to creating your product.

Some of the more inventive product managers have discovered lots of shipping containers for parts that are used by their products. With help from the rest of the company, they've gone ahead and shipped the packing material back to the sending company for reuse.

There are lots of different ways to make your product go green. Remember the three R's to the process: reduce, reuse, and recycle. It's always better to reduce or eliminate instead of reusing. It's always better to reuse instead of recycling. Finally, it's better to recycle than to send material to a landfill. Go green!

Chapter 5

Product Managers Know That EVERYBODY Must Be Green

Chapter 5: Product Managers Know That EVERYBODY Must Be Green

Product managers who decide to turn their products "green" in order to make less of an environmental impact need to **look beyond their own shop**. The initial challenge in taking a product green is to get the processes that you control to become more environmentally sensitive. The next step is to look at your suppliers.

How Far Does A Product Manager Have To Look?

Final assembly is what most product managers are involved in. No matter whether it's a router or a shrink-wrapped piece of software, generally a product manager is only responsible for the last few steps. However, innovative product managers know to look farther.

Your **suppliers** often have an enormous capability to improve your product's green image. However, as a product manager you have to convince them to do so. The simplest way to do this is to make it part of the initial supplier selection process.

Getting suppliers to participate will also require a product manager to marshal internal forces. This will include shipping & receiving as well as **finance** in order to confirm that the supplier has gone green and that any cost changes end up saving the company money in the long run.

That's Not Waste, That's A Product!

One green area where a product manager is especially well-suited to proving help is in determining what to do with the waste that is produced by his / her product. A great example of this can be found at a Subaru plant in Indiana where **a wall of water** is used to catch paint that misses a car as it is painted. The paint lands on the racing water, falls to the floor and is then separated from the water and reused.

Going Green IS A Competitive Advantage

In the end, the main reason that any Product Manger would go green needs to be because it provides his / her product with a **competitive advantage**. This advantage can be gotten in two different ways: cost savings and regulatory advantage. Going green should cut down on waste and scrap, this will directly improve your product's contribution to the company's bottom line. Additionally, as **global regulations** regarding waste and recycling become more and more strict, already having a green product is a key advantage.

Chapter 6

What A Pastry Store Can Teach Product Managers

Chapter 6: What A Pastry Store Can Teach Product Managers

Product Managers all over the place are asking the same question: what should I be doing to **boost my product sales** during this extend economic downturn? If you read the papers and the trade magazines, there are no shortage of "experts" who are more than willing to offer their suggestions. I prefer to listen to product managers who are actually taking action and seeing real results.

A Delicious Product & A Sticky Problem

Anjali Cordeiro over at the Dow Jones Newswires has been out looking for folks who are **finding ways to adjust their product to fit the new economic reality**. Cordeiro found Gary Gottenbusch who is not only the product manager, but also the owner of the Servatil Pastry Shop & Deli in Cincinnati.

What could a pastry shop have to teach an important product manager like you? Well, in early 2008 Gottenbusch started to see his customers beginning to buy smaller items in an effort to **conserve money** and at the same time his cost of materials was starting to **go through the roof**. Does this sound familiar?

Baking Up A New Business Plan

Gottenbusch was smart enough to realize that if he took a defensive approach and shrunk his product lines in an effort to just make it through the economic downturn, then there was a good chance he'd go out of business if it lasted too long. Instead, he seized the opportunity and **reinvented his product lines** and how he sold them.

Gottenbush did four things that every product manager should be doing right now:

1. He went looking for **new customers** in new locations.

2. He created **new and unique products** that would drive more traffic to his business.

3. He did creative things to keep his **costs under control**.

4. He took advantage of these unique times to **expand his business**.

Was it worth it? Well his sales are up by **15%** and he's now moving **$8.5M** worth of pastries per year. Let's look at exactly what he did...

Ingredients Of A Success Story

Realizing that volume is the key to keeping a product line successful during tough times, Gottenbusch went looking for new customers. He found them in **hospitals** where both patients and their friends and families are looking for something better than what you can get out of a vending machine.

Gottenbusch created a **unique pretzel stick** that he patented. He heavily promoted this product and used it to drive new customers to his store. The product sold well and had the added benefit that people who bought it often also bought his other products.

Keeping costs under control was a bit tougher. Gottenbusch joined forces with other bakers and they started **buying supplies in bulk**. This allowed them to get better prices than if they were buying individually. Prices kept going up, but they were much more manageable with the power of group buying.

Finally, since the economy is in the dumps, Gottenbusch used this as an opportunity to **buy store space** in a high-end mall that he normally couldn't have afforded to get into and is now selling his products there.

What Success Tastes Like

What should product managers learn from all of this? Simple – even in these tough times, it is still possible for your product to be a success. However, you can't be standing still. You need to be taking innovative action and this just might include changing your business model.

This is the time to be trying new things. You need to make sure that your customers see your product offerings as being unique and offering special value to them. If you get creative now, then when this recession is over you and your products will be well positioned to take advantage of the rebound.

Chapter 7

Product Manager Lessons From An Online Company In China

Chapter 7: Product Manager Lessons From An Online Company In China

Times are tough. Times are tough all over. This just happens to include China. Over there, one of China's most prominent **web-based companies** is taking some innovative steps to deal with the current global recession. What they are doing to stay successful holds a lot of lessons for product managers everywhere.

When Things Get Tight...

Loretta Chao over at the Wall Street Journal reports that Alibaba.com provides a fairly simple service to their customers: they are sorta like a Chinese version of Ebay for businesses. They provide **product listings** on their site for Chinese firms that want to export goods and they provide translation services for firms that want to buy Chinese goods.

Back in 1Q08, they started to notice that their core manufacturing customers were **starting to delay** membership renewals and that the number of new members who were signing up was dropping off.

The Solution

So what did Alibaba do? The company's business model operates by charging sellers for having listings on their site and for other services. The company responded to the downturn by **cutting prices** for the kind of customers that make up the core of their business. Additionally, they created a new program to help their customers **find loans** that would see them through the current financial crisis.

The Results

Immediately after introducing the new pricing scheme, Alibaba experienced 12,000 new paying members. This was **10x** the number of members who had bought the package at the higher price in the previous 9 months.

The new pricing was put in place by creating a new category of customer: they get to purchase a "starter-pack" subscription that has fewer services than their main product, but its price is also **60% lower** than the standard product's price.

The Bottom Line

Yes, this new product offering is **putting the squeeze on Alibaba's profit margins**. They were at about 45% last year and now they are hovering at 27.7%. Additionally, some existing customers have chosen to renew their memberships at the new lower rate (with fewer features).

However, most analysts agree that by changing its business model, Alibaba is now well positioned to grow its market share and become **bigger and stronger** when the economic slowdown is over.

Chapter 8

Performance Based Pricing – Is It Right For Product Managers In Tough Times?

Chapter 8: Performance Based Pricing – Is It Right For Product Managers In Tough Times?

Not to get too doom and gloom on you or anything, but how is your product doing these days? Sales a bit down? Sales fallen off a cliff? Desperate times call for desperate measures and I'm willing to bet that you are starting to get some pressure from upstairs / sales to start slashing your product's price.

Don't do it! Pricing is a complex beast and if you start slashing, you're not going to be able to raise it once things get better. I've got a different approach for you to take – try **performance based pricing.**

What NOT To Do In Bad Times

I'm not sure about you, but in my experience when the good ship business starts to run into stormy waters, the first thing the captain wants to throw overboard are **the advertising and marketing programs** (to which product managers are firmly attached). Clearly, communicating with the customer is seen as an unaffordable luxury.

Can you tell that I think that this is a VERY bad idea? After those budgets have been given the old heave-ho, the crazed captain and his crew start looking at your **product's price** as a heavy weight that must be gotten rid of if the firm is to make it through the storm.

In these desperate times, what nobody seems to remember is that if you dramatically lower the price of your product, you will have done two **potentially fatal** things to your product from which it may never recover.

The first is that you've now **cut any profit** that your product has been bringing in. This is pretty much like drilling a hole in the company boat. Now not only do you have to worry about the economic storm swamping the boat, but you've got red ink flooding in to the lower compartments and you not having a bailing bucket.

Finally, can anyone take just a moment and think about what a very low price for your product is going to **communicate to your customer**? The low quality / diluted brand effect is going to be like a sailor's tattoo – you won't be able to remember where you got it, but it's always there.

A Different Way: Performance Based Pricing

Difficult times require innovative thinking – put down your PowerPoint slides and get your calculator out. What this means for you is that instead of slashing your prices, perhaps it would be better to **do away with your existing pricing model all together**. How's that for out-of-the-box thinking?

What we're talking about here is moving from a fixed price scheme like you have today to a **performance based pricing scheme**. This approach is best suited to product managers who have **service based products**, but with a little creative thinking it can be applied to almost any product.

Performance based pricing calls for you to **stop charging your customer up-front** for the full price of the product. You may still charge them some smaller fee to cover processing the order and perhaps shipping and installation. However, in these hard times their up-front charges will be dramatically reduced.

Fear not – your product has not become a charitable gift. Rather, **your contract with your customer** now reflects a sharing between your two firms of the benefits that your customer will receive from using the product. Ah, how's that for a switch?

The Devil Is In The Details

As you can probably imagine, just **how that contract gets written** is the key to your product's and your firm's long term success with performance-based pricing. Almost all of the risk in this setup now lies on your shoulders...

There are **three** key performance-based pricing considerations that you need to keep in mind when you are working out the contract details with your customer:

- **Stick With Customers That You Know**: A pricing scheme like this needs to be used with customers that are operating in industries that you know something about. That new customer who is developing that tidal wave powered fuel cell is probably a poor candidate.

- **Define "Success"**: Your customer is buying your product to accomplish some very specific thing. Do you know what that is? Do they? Working out an agreement as to what "success" looks like is critical to making this type of pricing work.

- **Control The Variables**: Even if you both agree as to what success looks like, there are many other things that can get in the way of your customer achieving it. You need to lock down the possible variables that can allow your customer to claim that success was not achieved.

Final Thoughts

When you are awakened in the night by the ship's captain who tells you that the boat is going down and your product's pricing is too heavy and needs to be thrown overboard, remember that **you've got options**. In my experience, rash pricing decisions made quickly at the end of all-day strategy sessions always come back to haunt you.

Performance-based pricing is one pricing tool that you have that just might **allow you to emerge from this economic storm** with your product's brand intact. This is how great product managers make their product(s) **fantastically successful**.

Chapter 9

Going Cheap Is Ok For Some Product Managers

Chapter 9: Going Cheap Is Ok For Some Product Managers

Ok, I'll say it one more time: times are tough all over. If you are a Product Manager whose product is, how shall I say this nicely, priced on the **high side** then what are you to do in these troubling times?

Sure you can mess around with your products pricing and you could even consider launching another lower priced product line if you were so inclined. However, sometimes that's just **not possible**. What then product manager?

Creatively Offering Less Expensive Products

This is one of those discussions that if we don't get grounded real quickly we're going to end up flying off into the either and I'll just be talking to myself. So just for a minute, let's pretend that you are the product manager who is responsible for **Ferrari cars** at an auto dealership – no you don't make 'em, but you do control the marketing mix.

Right now there are three new "hot" Ferrari models: F430, 599, and 612 Scaglietti. But of course it is a **down economy** Mr. Ferrari dealership product manager. What are you going to do?

The **F430** is going to put your customers back about $218,000, the **599** will cost them roughly $320,000, and the **612** will put them back $313,000. Let's not even talk about tax, tags, and dealer prep costs!

Hopefully it goes without saying that the Ferrari F430 is your **bargain product** here. In troubling times, when people go out to buy a Ferrari it sure seems like they'll be picking up more F430s than other models. This is an important fact for any product manager to realize.

Only Make What You Can Sell

What our Ferrrari example is designed to help us understand is that one additional tool that a product manager has in his / her pocket is the ability to control **your mix of products** that you offer to your customers. If you were controlling what Ferraris a dealership presented to its customers you'd start stocking more F430's and fewer 599's and 612's.

Now a small point of subtlety is required here. At our fictitious Ferrari dealership, we **WILL** be having some folks come in who are flush with cash and will want to buy an upper end 599 or 612. Fantastic! Let's make sure that we've got a couple of those on hand so that we can take care of them and then stock the rest of the dealership with F430s.

Final Thoughts

I'm not a product manager responsible for stocking a Ferrari dealership; however, how cool would that be? Even if we are responsible for less glamorous products right now, the **lessons learned** apply to us also.

Right now most of our customers are trying to conserve money so they will be looking for lower priced products. If you are responsible for controlling the mix of products (or product configurations) presented to your customers, then you need to **increase the low end and minimize the high end** for now. At the same time, you need to realize that you'll always have the occasional high end buyer and so you need to be ready to service them when they show up. This is how great product managers make their product(s) **fantastically successful**.

Chapter 10

New Coke: A Product Manager Campfire Story

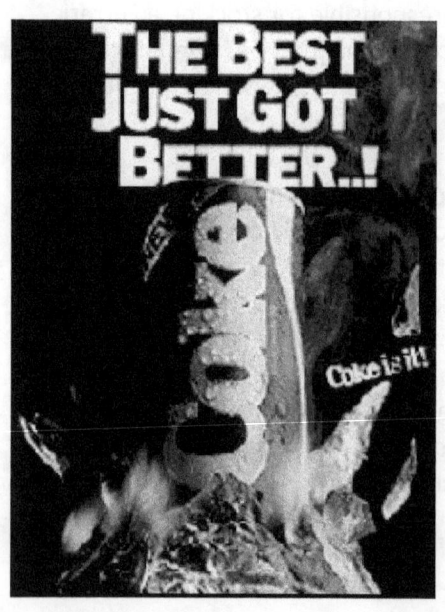

Chapter 10: New Coke: A Product Manager Campfire Story

In the world of product managers there are a few stories that the old hands talk about when they get together. The product failures, the flubs, and the downright fiascos that have grown into legends that are now only mentioned in hushed tones when a product manager is trying to kill a product idea that he / she knows will doom a product. One such story is the tale of **New Coke**.

What Was New Coke?

You young whipper-snapper product managers out there might not be familiar with the story of New Coke, so we probably should go all the way back to **the beginning** – April 23, 1985.

The Coca-Cola Company had a problem back in the early 1980's: people were telling Coke that they liked **the sweeter taste of Pepsi** better than the taste of Coke. Being a careful company who didn't like to rush into anything, Coke spent the years from 1981 to 1984 taste testing both a new and the old formulas of Coke. They ended up doing this over **200,000** times in **25** different cities.

What Coke's Customers Told Them

The results of the taste tests were very clear to Coke's product managers: **55%** of the people tested preferred the taste of New Coke **over** the old formula. You might think that people made this selection because they didn't know what they were drinking. However, the product managers at Coke thought of this also – in the taste tests that they performed where the person knew which sample was New Coke and which was the old formula, people's preference for New Coke shot up by an additional **6%**!

What Happened When New Coke Was Introduced?

On April 23, 1985 Coke announced that they were going to **stop making Coke using the old formula** and from then on only make New Coke. Boom! The world blew up overnight – at least in terms of Coke drinkers. People overwhelmed Coke's customer support phone lines by calling to complain, they filed lawsuits to **stop the switchover** (which got dismissed), they said that they'd never buy Coke again, etc. Clearly the Coke product managers had made a huge mistake...

What Did Coke Do Wrong? (The Scarcity Principle)

So what did Coke do wrong here? Simple – they forgot about **The Scarcity Principle**. During those taste tests where people knew which sample was New Coke and which was the old formula, they also knew that they couldn't get New Coke at that time and so they naturally showed a stronger preference for **what they couldn't have**.

Coke probably thought that the 6% increase in desire for New Coke when people knew which sample was which meant that customers had a higher desire for something new. However, they were wrong.

When Coke replaced the old formula with New Coke, what happened is that people's desire for the old formula shot up because now it was **the thing that they could no longer have**. That's what caused the riots.

Final Thoughts

One of the best-supported findings in social science is that customers are **more sensitive to possible losses** than to possible gains. In this case, when Coke announced that they were going to stop making old formula Coke, this was a much bigger deal to Coke drinkers than the general availability of New Coke.

Product managers spend a lot of time listing out all of the benefits of their new products in the hopes of capturing new customers or getting existing customers to trade up. We all need to learn from the story of New Coke that sometimes our customers may **have become so attached to our existing product** that possibility of losing their existing product far outweighs the benefits of our new product. Being aware of this is how great product managers make their product(s) **fantastically successful**.

Chapter 11

Cost Of Materials Is A Product Manager's New Friend

Chapter 11: Cost Of Materials Is A Product Manager's New Friend

In the current tough economic times we are all feeling the pressure to keep sales of our product either at current levels or to boost them in order to make up for shortfalls in other parts of the company. When you step back for a moment and realize that our customers, both current and potential, are also feeling the squeeze of tight times, how will a product manager pull off this **magic trick**?

How To Reduce Your Product's Costs

This is going to be a very simple lesson (with a lot of explanations to follow): use less costly materials to reduce the cost of your product. We all realize that the cost of one of our products is heavily dependent on **what it took to build it**; however, sometimes we're too close to the product to be able to see how these costs can be reduced.

As they teach us in product manager school (you did go to that, didn't you?) there are two types of costs that go in each unit of your product that is created. Note that this applies to both "real" (you can touch 'em) and "service" products. The first type of cost is called a **"fixed"** cost – it doesn't matter if you manufacture one or a million units your fixed costs will always remain the same. We're talking about things like salaries for managers, lighting, air conditioning for plants and warehouses, etc. Then there are **"variable"** costs which are the cost of producing one more unit. This would be the cost of plastic, or a circuit board, or a nice steak (if you were running a restaurant & selling meals).

To cut your costs, you need to find ways to **reduce** both your fixed and variable costs.

About Those Fixed Costs

The tricky thing about a product's fixed costs is that all too often we take a quick look at them, shrug our shoulders, and say that there's **nothing that we can do** about them. It turns out that this isn't true.

Fixed costs are often established when we first start to make and sell a product. Rarely do we go back and **revisit them** when everything is humming along nicely. Have you looked at the economy lately? There are three fixed cost factors that you need to be revisiting right now:

- **Manufacturing – Site:** where does your product get created? Does it need to be made there – are there less expensive alternatives? Now may be a good time to renegotiate your site costs.

- **Manufacturing – Tools:** how does your product get made? No matter if it's being done by people or machines, looking for ways to use fewer of either can be a big bottom line savings technique.

- **Storage**: where do you put your manufactured products after they've been created and before they've been sold? How much is this costing you? Once again this is a great time to renegotiate these types of contracts.

They're Called Variable Costs For A Reason

The real savings in making a product generally comes from finding ways to reduce your variable costs. This makes sense because every penny you can shave off of a variable cost will be saved **over and over again** each time you make another unit. Things you should be looking at to reduce variable costs include:

- **Housings**: most products are enclosed in some sort of housing. This can often be one of your most significant product production costs. Often this component has been over-engineered. Can you make it thinner or make it out of different materials while still keeping acceptable product quality?

- **Packing Material**: when you ship / deliver your product how do you pack it? Once again, packing solutions are often designed once and then not revisited as improvements in shipping materials and methods are developed. This is a good time to take another look at this area.

- **Rework**: One of the most expensive parts of any manufacturing process is the extra level of effort that is required to solve special issues that occur while the product is being manufactured. Spending some time to reduce the amount of rework can pay huge dividends.

Final Thoughts

Tough times offer product managers the excuse that they may have been looking for to **revisit both the fixed and variable costs** associated with their product. However, cutting costs is not all that a product manager needs to do.

In order to maintain profits, product managers also need to find ways to increase their sales. If you can reduce your product's costs, then you'll have more pricing flexibility and that will allow you to boost your sales. This is how great product managers make their product(s) **fantastically successful**.

Chapter 12

Slimmed Down Products Make Product Managers Look Good

Chapter 12: Slimmed Down Products Make Product Managers Look Good

If product managers ran the world, we'd be able to sell our products to **everyone** at a **very high price**. However, since we don't run the world (yet), we need to adjust and adapt in order to sell our products to as many people as possible for as high a price as is possible. However, when the global economy tanks, we've got **a whole new set of challenges** that we've got to deal with...

Slimming Down Your Product

When your customer have less money to spend, you've got to adjust how your product "looks" to them in order to get and hold their attention. Taking a large, expensive product or service and **"slimming it down"** can make it more attractive to your customers who are price-conscious.

This approach works best for product managers who are **managing services** such as marketing firms, design firms, etc. A good example would be a firm that does landscape design. Instead of selling a complete redesign of a yard, perhaps they could slim this product down and offer a consulting package that includes a site visit, a discussion about wants and needs, and a preliminary design. As always, this can be a great lead-in to a larger sale later.

Unbundling Your Product

For those of us product managers who have products, not services to manage, a different tact can be taken. Take a hard look at your product as it stands today. Is there any way that you can take that product and **"unbundle"** it – basically break it into separate components? If you can find a way to do this, then you can turn around and start to sell the components separately.

The good folks who sell us **cell phones** learned this trick a long time ago. Batteries, carrying cases, earphones, etc. are all sold separately (and at higher prices!)

Product Manager Beware!

One side benefit of unbundling a product is that a slimmed down product has the ability to **attract new customers**. However, all too often product managers start to dream about upselling new customers on additional products and thereby boosting their sales. This generally doesn't work because those new customers are simply looking for the slimmed down product and will go away if they don't find it.

Final Thoughts

Slimming down / unbundling existing products are a great way for product managers to help their companies make it through tough times. However, you need to remember that times won't always be this tough. That means that you've got to very clear about what your customers are going to be able to get at what price.

Customers associate **price with value** and that means that that they'll understand that they will be getting less at a lower price. Make sure to leave the door open to offering more at a higher price later on. Follow these suggestions and you will have found out how great product managers make their product(s) **fantastically successful**.

It's from the forge of failure that the steel of success is formed.

Hard Work Does Not Guarantee Success, But Success Does Not Happen Without Hard Work.

- Dr. Jim Anderson

Create Products Your Customers Want At A Price That They Are Willing To Pay!

Dr. Jim Anderson is available to provide training and coaching on the two topics that are the most important to product managers everywhere: how do I create the products that my customers want and what should I price them at?

Dr. Anderson believes that in order to both learn and remember what he says, product managers need to laugh. Each one of his speeches is full of fun and humor so that what he says "sticks" with everyone.

Dr. Anderson's Product Management Training Includes:

1. How can you segment your market?
2. What problems are your customers having right now?
3. Which of your customer's problems does your product solve?
4. How much of this problem does your product solve?
5. How much will it cost your customer if they don't fix this problem?

Dr. Jim Anderson presents over 100 speeches per year. To invite Dr. Anderson to speak at your event, contact him at:

Phone: 813-418-6970 or
Email: jim@BlueElephantConsulting.com

Blue Elephant Consulting

Speaking Negotiating Managing Marketi

Photo Credits:

Cover - Sherman Geronimo-Tan
https://www.flickr.com/photos/smanography/

Chapter 1 - Michael Taggart Photography
https://www.flickr.com/photos/michael_harold/

Chapter 2 – Jeffrey
https://www.flickr.com/photos/jb912/

Chapter 3 - Kevin Dooley
https://www.flickr.com/photos/pagedooley/

Chapter 4 - City of York Council UK
https://www.flickr.com/photos/yorkcouncil/

Chapter 5 - Maryland GovPics
https://www.flickr.com/photos/mdgovpics/

Chapter 6 - jpellgen
https://www.flickr.com/photos/jpellgen/

Chapter 7 - Andy Mitchell
https://www.flickr.com/photos/monstermunch/

Chapter 8 - Defence Images
https://www.flickr.com/photos/defenceimages/

Chapter 9 - Paul§
https://www.flickr.com/photos/87338661@N08/

Chapter 10 - Archie McPhee
https://www.flickr.com/photos/archiemcpheeonline/

Chapter 11 - Alden Jewell
https://www.flickr.com/photos/autohistorian/

Chapter 12 – Dr. Jim Anderson

Other Books By The Author

Product Management

- What Product Managers Need To Know About World-Class Product Development: How Product Managers Can Create Successful Products

- How Product Managers Can Learn To Understand Their Customers: Techniques For Product Managers To Better Understand What Their Customers Really Want

- Product Management Secrets: Techniques For Product Managers To Boost Product Sales And Increase Customer Satisfaction

- Product Development Lessons For Product Managers: How Product Managers Can Create Successful Products

- Customer Lessons For Product Managers: Techniques For Product Managers To Better Understand What Their Customers Really Want

- Product Failure Lessons For Product Managers: Examples Of Products That Have Failed For Product

Managers To Learn From

- Communication Skills For Product Managers: The Communication Skills That Product Managers Need To Know How To Use In Order To Have A Successful Product

- How To Have A Successful Product Manager Career: The Things That You Need To Be Doing TODAY In Order To Have A Successful Product Manager Career

- Product Manager Product Success: How to keep your product on track and make it become a success

Public Speaking

- Tools Speakers Need In Order To Give The Perfect Speech: What tools to use to create your next speech so that your message will be remembered forever!

- How To Create A Speech That Will Be Remembered

- Secrets To Organizing A Speech For Maximum Impact: How to put together a speech that will capture and hold your audience's attention

- How To Become A Better Speaker By Changing How You Speak: Change techniques that will transform a speech into a memorable event

- How To Give A Great Presentation: Presentation techniques that will transform a speech into a memorable event

- How To Rehearse In Order To Give The Perfect Speech: How to effectively rehearse your next speech to that your message be remembered forever!

- Secrets To Creating The Perfect Speech: How to create a speech that will make your message be remembered forever!

- Secrets To Organizing The Perfect Speech: How to organize the best speech of your life!

- Secrets To Planning The Perfect Speech: How to plan to give the best speech of your life

- How To Show What You Mean During A Presentation: How to use visual techniques to transform a speech into a memorable event

CIO Skills

- Becoming A Powerful And Effective Leader: Tips And Techniques That IT Managers Can Use In Order To Develop Leadership Skills

- CIO Secrets For Growing Innovation: Tips And Techniques For CIOs To Use In Order To Make Innovation Happen In Their IT Department

- Your Success As A CIO Depends On How Well You Communicate: Tips And Techniques For CIOs To Use In Order To Become Better Communicators

- What CIOs Need To Know About Working With Partners: Techniques For CIOs To Use In Order To Be Able To Successfully Work With Partners

- Critical CIO Management Skills: Decision Making Skills That Every CIO Needs To Have In Order To Be Able To Make The Right Choices

- How CIOs Can Make Innovation Happen: Tips And Techniques For CIOs To Use In Order To Make Innovation Happen In Their IT Department

- CIO Communication Skills Secrets: Tips And Techniques For CIOs To Use In Order To Become Better Communicators

- Managing Your CIO Career: Steps That CIOs Have To Take In Order To Have A Long And Successful Career

- CIO Business Skills: How CIOs can work effectively with the rest of the company!

IT Manager Skills

- Save Yourself, Save Your Job – How To Manage Your IT Career: Secrets That IT Managers Can Use In Order To Have A Successful Career

- Growing Your CIO Career: How CIOs Can Work With The Entire Company In Order To Be Successful

- How IT Managers Can Make Innovation Happen: Tips And Techniques For IT Managers To Use In Order To Make Innovation Happen In Their Teams

- Staffing Skills IT Managers Must Have: Tips And Techniques That IT Managers Can Use In Order To Correctly Staff Their Teams

- Secrets Of Effective Leadership For IT Managers: Tips And Techniques That IT Managers Can Use In Order To Develop Leadership Skills

- IT Manager Career Secrets: Tips And Techniques That IT Managers Can Use In Order To Have A Successful Career

- IT Manager Budgeting Skills: How IT Managers Can Request, Manage, Use, And Track Their Funding

- Secrets Of Managing Budgets: What IT Managers Need To Know In Order To Understand How Their Company Uses Money

Negotiating

- Learn How To Signal In Your Next Negotiation: How To Develop The Skill Of Effective Signaling In A Negotiation In Order To Get The Best Possible Outcome

- Learn The Skill Of Exploring In A Negotiation: How To Develop The Skill Of Exploring What Is Possible In A Negotiation In Order To Reach The Best Possible Deal

- Learn How To Argue In Your Next Negotiation: How To Develop The Skill Of Effective Arguing In A Negotiation In Order To Get The Best Possible Outcome|

- How To Open Your Next Negotiation: How To Start A Negotiation In Order To Get The Best Possible Outcome

- Preparing For Your Next Negotiation: What You Need To Do BEFORE A Negotiation Starts In Order To Get The Best Possible Deal

- Learn How To Package Trades In Your Next Negotiation

- All Good Things Come To An End: How To Close A Negotiation - How To Develop The Skill Of Closing In Order To Get The Best Possible Outcome From A Negotiation

- Take No Prisoners In Your Next Negotiation: How To Start A Negotiation In Order To Get The Best Possible Outcome

Miscellaneous

- The Internet-Enabled Successful School District Superintendent: How To Use The Internet To Boost Parental Involvement In Your Schools

- Power Distribution Unit (PDU) Secrets: What Everyone Who Works In A Data Center Needs To

Know!

- Making The Jump: How To Land Your Dream Job When You Get Out Of College!

- How To Use The Internet To Create Successful Students And Involved Parents

Techniques For Product Managers To Boost Product Sales And Increase Customer Satisfaction

> This book has been written with one goal in mind – to show you how to manage your product. No matter if it's setting the right price, creating a product vision, or dealing with name changes we'll show you how to do it correctly
>
> **Let's Make Your Product A Success!**

What You'll Find Inside:

- **PRODUCT MANAGERS KNOW THAT EVERYBODY MUST BE GREEN**
- **WHAT A PASTRY STORE CAN TEACH PRODUCT MANAGERS**
- **PERFORMANCE BASED PRICING – IS IT RIGHT FOR PRODUCT MANAGERS IN TOUGH TIMES?**
- **NEW COKE: A PRODUCT MANAGER CAMPFIRE STORY**

Dr. Jim Anderson brings over 25 years of real-world product management experience to this book. He's managed products at some of the world's largest firms as well as at start-ups. He's going to show you what you need to do in order to make your career a success!

www.ingramcontent.com/pod-product-compliance
Lightning Source LLC
Chambersburg PA
CBHW060421190526
45169CB00002B/1001